I0616297

A COLLECTION OF POEMS

Taking Notes

A Mother's Healing Journey Through Grief

LEE A. GLASSCOCK

Copyright © 2025 Lee A. Glasscock

All rights reserved. No portion of this book may be reproduced by any process or technique without the express permission of the publisher or author, except for purposes of promotion in which excerpts, not to exceed three lines, may be reprinted. Please notify Cairn Press when reprinting any portion of this text.

All inquiries should be directed to: cairnpressbooks@gmail.com.

Cairn Press Books
3438 Emmorton Road, #4
Abingdon, MD 21009
443-356-6367

Paperback ISBN: 979-8-218-66153-3
eBook ISBN: 979-8-218-66921-8
Library of Congress Control Number: 2025908486

Cover Design: Jean Merrill & Ranilo Cabo
Layout: Ranilo Cabo
Editor and Proofreader: Karen Burton
Book Midwife: Carrie Jareed

CAIRN PRESS
Guideposts for Your Journey!

In loving memory of Carrie, my beloved daughter
Forever my soul mate, my heart, my connection to God
with gratitude for all she continues to teach me

Our sorrows and wounds are healed only when we touch them with compassion.
—Buddha

Contents

Introduction

My life, as I had known it, ended one afternoon in 2011. I returned home to find not only my husband's car, but my daughter and son-in-law's car in the drive. At first, delighted, I thought my dear ones were gathered awaiting my return—what a joyous surprise for an afternoon! But as I entered our home, my husband took my hand and asked me to sit down. I looked from one loved one's face to the next as the terrible news was revealed—*it's back*.

Carrie was a loving daughter, wife, sister, daughter-in-law, dog mom, aunt, friend, and compassionate physician. She had originally been diagnosed with breast cancer at age thirty-one while she was a third-year medical student. Despite surgery and treatments, she graduated with honors in 2006. Her calling was caring for people, and when the cancer returned in 2011, she courageously went through more treatments, practicing medicine and supporting breast cancer research until she was no longer able. She then received palliative care, an area of medicine she was passionate about, believing strongly in the need for providing comfort and care to those who decide not to pursue treatment toward the end of life. She died at home in 2016, at age forty-two.

These are the details of her life and death, but Carrie was so much more—her compassion, her sense of humor, and beauty of spirit were her most remarkable traits, and she joyously shared those with others. Now she whispers to me those same gifts but from an unlimited perspective, hence the title *Taking Notes*. If you find comfort or hope in these poems, it's because Carrie wants you to find your way onto the healing path where she continues to guide me. Grief truly is a never-ending journey, but what I have found (and continue to find) is that it's also the path to healing.

I offer these poems from a place of deep gratitude for all the loving support I have received in my own healing journey. I believe that grief—felt in the marrow of our being—can be nurtured by that loving support and lead to spiritual growth. It can guide us to a deeper understanding of connection with ourselves, with others, with all of life.

I have learned grief is not a linear process. These poems begin in a place of raw grief. Yet, over time, my journey was enlightened by Carrie's spirit as she reached across the veil to share her love and joy, wrapping my broken heart in the unbounded light she now dwells in.

SECTION 1

The Beginning

Carrie

Your tender bravery reaches into my heart.
I'm by your side.
I hear your gracious words
    even those spoken to people
    whose eyes don't see the suffering behind your serene smile.

Your kindness abounds as you navigate your new reality.
You refuse to be defined by a disease.

I look closely with a mother's watchful eye. I see no contraction.
You turn up the corners of your mouth and meet fear with the
fortitude of a warrior
    a gentle warrior—
a heart bringing humor and warmth to your landscape.
You warm the lives you touch
    and they are many—
with unspeakable compassion.

Sorrow tempered the steel of your character.
Your strength—molded, formed
shines forth from your soul,
bringing light to others, including me.

I am proud to walk beside you.
I am blessed to answer when you say *Mom.*

Breathing Eternity

The grayness of the day
serves to heighten the greenness of the leaves,
tiny droplets of rain clinging to their tips.

I too cling to this moment—
this moment of great challenge
and greater love.
The news, now two weeks old,
brought me to my knees.

I ask Life—
What would you have me do?
What must I make of the ever-present Now?

There is no pre-marked path,
no hidden trail I must find, follow.
There is only Now, the living prayer,
the enormity of a life compressed
into a single second.

How vast
    how expansive
        how intense
when each breath is infused with eternity.

Yet fleeting as the hummingbird's flight—
stopping ever so briefly
    to drink nectar
        to taste simple sweetness
            to be nourished in a moment.

Can this be my prayer?
Can this be my answer?

Surrendering Everyday Sight

I stand in a pose of adoration,
opening a mother's eggshell heart.
I bring all my vulnerabilities
and lay them at the feet of the great Unknown.

I stand at the gate, broken open.
No name exists for what I feel.
The human tongue cannot form this prayer.

I place my fear in the cradle of loving kindness,
surrounding it in warmth,
releasing it from my body,
releasing it into the secret Source.

I kneel, forehead to sacred ground.
I surrender to the Oneness.
I place my mustard seed of faith on the great altar of Life,
raising my eyes and palms skyward.

I look into the Light and everyday sight falls away.

This life is my prayer, and I can live no other.
I entrust all that is mine into the loving arms of the great Spirit,
    and I am comforted.

Earth Birth

When you fought to emerge *sunny-side up*
were you praying for the cup to pass?
With the blood, sweat, and tears that came to our eyes,
did we somehow know the die was cast?

The journey began,
born of deep joy and great pain.
The sound of our cries shaking the earth
sent the healing rain.

We walked this path
heart in hand,
asking God for his plan,
knowing He has no wrath.

With each breath we drew,
Somehow, we knew
the cup would not pass.
We'd come to know the truth at last.

The gift would transcend,
we learned from within.
Life eternal goes on—
Love never ends.

A Note From God

Did I know when your form emerged from mine
that our mortal journey would be cut short in time?
That glorious day of your human birth—
a note from God, a sign, a key?
Your sojourn here on planet earth,
the word that Life's a mystery.

The waves were there along the way,
your spirit soared for its brief stay.
The lives you touched, the hearts you won—
it seemed your story had just begun.

Now you have moved to higher ground.
yet guide us through, no longer bound
by time or space or earthly coup.
Your eyes behold a brighter view.

You whisper smiles across the miles,
and tulips bloom in sweet delight.
We celebrate, our souls unite,
you've left us with a precious light,

Down on my knees, I kiss the ground.
The love you shared—forever found.

SECTION 2

Ragged Heart

The *Keening*

I am being consumed by fire—the longing of my soul for you.
Where can I rest my soul?
Where can I find you?
What heart can hold this pain?
Where is respite on this journey?

I ache for your laughter, to hear your voice ring out,
wash over me as a healing rain, a liquid balm to soothe and comfort.
Hold me, walk with me, wipe my tears.
You, you are my strength—
you are the one to lay open the core of my being.

How we danced this winding road!
No stone unturned—the joy, the sorrow, the grit, and pain—all of it.
I want all of it.
Every cell of my body mourns.

What offering can I lay at the feet of the divine to know that
    ferocious connection again?

I rock and keen, crying out for your touch.
The forsakenness is overwhelming.
Need consumes me.
Raw and ragged, I kneel before your memory.
Drained, yet not empty—
for your coming filled me so completely.
I have known God, the teacher of Love, to whom I will return.

Communion

God enters my heart only after I empty the tears of despair. My silent scream pours out from utter brokenness, even beyond prayer. The bleeding, the purging, the seemingly endless walk through hell seem to be the price of admission to resurrection and healing—ever-evolving, ever-presenting new facets of the Divine. Just when total darkness threatens to overwhelm my entire being, a tiny blade of spring green grass pokes through desolation. As the pangs of yet another birthing begin to subside, I look up and receive pure, infinite, and ever-abiding love. GOD IS!

Lovesight

Entwined in heart and mind
within a wisdom more powerful than all despair.
Like a plant, I face the sun.
Full of love, I see you—
   no longer blind.

Faith, she said

Faith, she said.
But does she know how to return
from the place of complete darkness—
from a barren soul?

I have walked with bloody feet
the road of loss that destroys.
My eyes beheld a sight
beyond the rupture of death.

Yesterday, I turned from this life,
I said goodbye to hope.
I stood on ravaged ground.
Today, I speak faith that *knows*.

Love's Grace

Sweet tears like a gentle rain,
peace settling into my heart.
The grace of love replaced the pain.
I see the way to do my part

Do what you do, she whispered to me.
Know you are never alone.
Look through your soul, then you will see
faith is guiding you home.

Another Sunday Morning

Oh gentle spirit, you are with me always.

But how I long for your smile,
your full body laugh.
Oh, to wrap my arms around you and hold you tight.
I feel your heart beat next to mine
and remember when we shared that beat.

I am so grateful you chose me to be your mom.

Hollow Places

Denser today, the cold snaps my skin. But more—memory of your attentive listening haunts the hallways of my heart. I see your smile shining across time, but my eyes drip the wetness that longs to quench my thirst so deep.

I miss you. That sacred space we shared in our embodied beings. The layered love of these physical forms that could embrace, laugh, cry, dance the tune of life. That mortal fullness, that human touch, that naked joy.

The Biology of Grief

The stars have fallen and rest on my shoulders.
The layers slip away, dropping effortlessly as I allow.
The turbulence of yesterday has dissolved,
puddling at my feet in glorious surrender.
Yet another facet of this precious life story emerges from its
shadowy sheath.

I see the biology of this process—
the thought comes forth like an apple suddenly ripened overnight.
I awoke to the wisdom, to light.
I cry the tears freely now,
such release, seeing through the pain.
The suffering relents, and I am open
to mourn the loss of my best friend,
fullheartedly.

In the space of a single breath

I breathe your sweet essence and linger in remembrance,
exhaling into the depths of sorrow
as I experience the void you left in my life.
I stay in that space, yet I know that with my next in-breath,
you will be my inspiration
      forever and always.

Grief's Offering

Hello Grief, come to walk with me this road. We've traveled far and wide—deep, low-winding pathways. You've held me along the way in your embrace. Your handmaiden, Sorrow, has carved a space within me—hollowed me out to my skin and beyond. Her knife, jagged and sharp, etched my very soul. Naked and raw, I bent to the ground, wailing into the dark night. Salty waters bathed my body, anointing me with life's deepest essence. Yes, Grief, you reach out your hand to invite those who will follow: to love what death can touch is a rending of the heart beyond pain.

And yet—to fully step into the flow of life, to dance this mortal existence with every ounce of our being, we must pass through this sacred suffering. We are fortified and our lives transformed, for we have borne witness to life's greatest gift; we have gained access to the infinite capacity for compassion. Life—radical, beautiful, unbounded, overflowing, and full—is the offering you leave in your wake.

Heart Tears

My heart tears
stuck in my throat today.
It took a lot of breathing
to exhale them up into my eyes
where they could spill over
onto my cheeks
and drip back
down to my chest
where my heart could
inhale them once again.

The Nearness of You

You send me tears to christen my pain,
Reminding me that your death is not in vain.
You've left behind a love so bright—
on even the darkest days, I find the light.

The ache is there, still painful and sore,
but your presence in my heart is so much more.
I call your name in the depths of my pain,
and feel your touch in my heart once again.

My inner eye sees your laughter and smiles—
together forever, no matter the miles.
Your gentle whispers caressing my ear,
You assure me, *have faith*; you are ever near.

Child of Mine

Oh child of mine
you are the deep
flowing through me
but you belong to God
the Universe of Life
the tears I cry at your seeming loss
are the waters of my soul
refreshing me, reminding me
there is no distance in love
you are every breath I take
with every heartbeat
my body floods with your presence
as I step into
the knowingness you reach out
to remind me we are always
and forever together . . .

My heart is big enough

to hold the happy
to hold the hurt
to hold . . .
     glistening stars at night
     dancing diamonds on the sunlit sea
     the giggles of playing children
     birdsong in early morning dew
     a friend's welcoming smile
     a rose's sweet smell
     the memory of my nana's scent
     my babies' breath, soft on my cheek
     excitement as my love enters
     late-night book discussions with Mom
     pride as my kids grew into themselves
     and even the loss no parent can bear
and yet. . .
here is my heart—
     big enough to hold it all.

Prism of Oneness

Today my soul is sore, yearning for reunion.
The weariness of separation, the pain of loss walks close.
My heart is heavy.
And yet, the still, small voice whispers:
    You are on your spiritual path.
    Separation is an illusion
    for even the raindrop
    with its unique light, returns to the vast ocean,
    freely expressing its beautiful color
    as the prism of Oneness shines through.

Tender Sadness

Jagged edges of turbulent peaks and valleys soften
the dance with grief grows fluid
the motion gentler—
patience leading and guiding the journey
consoling my heart with mercy and compassion
the fierce grip lessening its hold,
creating space for inner peace
creating the ability to hold joy and sadness
together in my center and know
all is well

SECTION 3

Mending

Sweet Song of Life

She came.

She opened
 my body
 my heart
 my soul.

A tiny seed
she grew
she bloomed
she lit my life
she said
 I cannot sing.

Yet she hums
my truth
reaching across the veil
wrapping me
 in her voice.

Sweet song of life
she teaches the words—
 I listen.

What do I hear?
soundless whisper
a still lake
rippling messages
 across time, space

My ground of being
perfect stillness
—in motion—
the drop merges
back to source
 knowing itself divine.

Reunion

I held your micro-essence in my body
and now you wait, a breath away
for my journey from separation to reunion.

How could we ever be apart when
I carried you under my heart?

My Daughter

You walk on water now, my daughter
You travel on light beams as yet unseen
You move through the ether on a breath
You dance the eternal beyond time

In moments of stillness, I feel you
In the quiet, you speak
In my heart, you give me peace
In my soul, you heal me

Good-Bye?

Center of my soul.
Sunlight of my spirit.
We have never said good-bye.
How could we?

The Onion

Grief is like an onion.
As I release the outer skins
   —there is lightness.
Penetrating deeper layers
a tender sweetness surfaces,
yet sometimes a sharp edge catches in my heart
   —bringing tears to my eyes.
The deeper the layers, the more concentrated the essence.
Approaching the God center, merging into oneness,
the grief transfigures from loss to union . . .

Make space for Grace.

Yet, Here You Are*

Burning brightly, vanishing
in a life of early tears
Yet, here you are.

In our midst,
laughing your love all over us.
Your full body hugs draw us close,
sweet sips of joy as we hold you in our hearts,
recalling your passionate run on earth.

You must've known all along,
grabbing with gusto the juiciness of it all.
Your soul donned the exquisite costume
glistening with star dust,
dropping diamonds as you danced your way across our sky.

We gather to celebrate, wrapping each other
in our happy sadness,
filling cups from the fountain of you
    divinely human
    perfectly crafted
    a painfully brief time in this world.
How could you leave us?
Yet, here you are.

*Our Heaven Birthday Celebration of nearest and dearest to mark the
fifth anniversary of Carrie's passing

Reclamation

I have lost your physical presence in my life. That is a fact and yet, look at what I am reclaiming. I know in the depths of my soul you have found your voice. You sing to me from the trees, donning the colorful song of the brilliant red cardinal. I feel your gentle touch as the breeze moves through the trees—their leaves are so exhilaratingly green, I can smell them with my eyes. The ground beneath my feet is solid and firm, holding me as I reach for the sky to touch the cotton-ball clouds. Each day you beckon me into the fullness of this mortal life, so I drink deeply from the well of my earthly senses, all the while knowing we'll soar together again when I, too, return to the light.

I Taste Your Beauty in my Tears

The pores of my spirit yearn for your presence.
My memory transfigures your absence
as it grows more intense with time.
The sweet secret moments captured in my heart
bring you into my *now*.
   I sense you beyond mortality
   I drink your essence
   I taste your beauty in my tears
   I hear your laughter in the sounds of the sea.
Your eyes twinkle in the sky,
your light shining on through my love. . .
Forever.

The Alchemy of Her Leaving

She gave me a broken heart! I never asked for one. She carved her leaving path through me like the *jaws of life* extracting me from a crash. Now she births within me a love so deep at times I cannot breathe. In her passing, she changed me—left me torn apart yet made whole, bereft and somehow filled with all the precious pieces of her life yet unlived.

How can I express how she urges me to pass on to the world all she has to give? Propelling me to listen deeply, breathing into my soul the expansiveness of her being, the radiance she pours into me when I open. Like an alchemist, she forces me into the fire. Burning with the pain of her passing, I melt into nothingness until what is left is transformed. The jagged edges of my sorrow dissolve in the crucible of holy darkness to cool and emerge tempered and glistening in the new light of awareness. I am so full I think I will explode into a million pieces and fly off into the infinity of I know not what.

How can this be contained in a human heart?
—the formless condensing into form and then the unbirthing of a soul?
—the Divine drawing back its own unto itself?
—the inhalation of eternity as it enfolds all that has been created?
—the end?

God exhales and the world bursts forth again. This is the gift she gives, this glimpse into the mystery of it all, this stream of light, this vantage point of grace to know it is all perfect just as it is.

You and the Moon

Sliver of silver, hung in the sky,
is it true, can it be?
I thought I said good-bye,
yet, you are the light I cannot see.

Stormy Weather

Even when there is stormy weather in my soul—
especially when there is stormy weather in my soul—
you reach across the veil to comfort me.
I know you have never left me, will never leave me.

Thank you, Beloved Child.

Still . . .

Knitting a lace shawl of love
to wrap my broken heart
knowing your spirit has gone
ahead and lights my path

Still . . .
some days my mother's body
reaches arms to take you
to rock and soothe
to hold your hand and walk beside you
to see light shining in your eyes
    with joy of a new discovery
to share a lunch, a laugh, a cry

I embrace the million moments of you
I carry that give me strength
that make me see you are here
everywhere—
Still . . .

You Are There

Dancing through flights of fancy
Or dark dreary days of despair—
    You are there.

Dreaming deep thoughts of intention
And full-bodied laughs without care—
    You are there.

Winging my way back to heaven
With a heart much lighter than air—
    You are there.

In the secret space of my soul
With a sweet song of mystery so fair—
    You are there.

I know I can never lose you
In the single breath we forever share—
    You are there.

Softening

The edges of the hole in my heart are softening, feathery wings are forming, creating a lift, drawing me upward, filling me with a light so bright it burns—cauterizing my wound, healing and sealing with the kiss of compassion—a love so deep and high I connect to heaven and earth with every beat of my broken heart, filled with the peace that passes understanding.

The Shadow of a Bee

I saw you in the shadow of a bee
so subtle and slight
almost beyond my sight
Yet I know you were smiling at me.

The whisper of your voice
as it moves across my heart
tells me we are never apart,
your presence always speaking of choice.

The veil grows thin
the clouds drift around
although without sound
I know you're inviting me in.

Our worlds, woven always together
though appearances say you have left
and at times my soul feels bereft.
Yet your wings soaring, send me a feather.

Come dance in the light
you sing from above
ever wrapping me in your love
and kissing me softly *Good Night*.

In the white dawn of morning

you come calling.
Your gentle smile touches my lips.
So softly I feel your presence.
A whisper away, you breathe into my heart,
I'll love you forever and always.

Ease

Lying in the soft green velvet moss
my heart overflowing, deeply touched
awake to my loss
yet loving you so much.

That I am full of your being
held in my soul
my eyes always seeing
you are healed and whole.

Here in this moment of ease
your beauty forever captured in time
filling my body with peace
you've made your courage mine.

And so it is . . .

The Beckoning

As I awaken from my beautiful sleep
my breathing is easy, peaceful and deep.
I see your blue eyes in cerulean skies
my heart relaxing, softly beating its sighs.

You beckon me onward in a heavenly dance
the grace of your being through sunlight enhanced.
I feel your laughter roll from a cloud
I surrender to love, my head deeply bowed.

Equilibrium

I seek the secret equilibrium
    where we meet.
In the still night your presence appears
    your beautiful light washes over me,
    bathing me in our divine connection,
    a shimmering silver umbilical cord —never severed.
Your blessedness spills into my heart.
I weep with joy, breathing your essence,
    the holy, perfect, transcendent moment of your birth,
    eternally *now*.

The Greatest Gift

Moonbeams and meteors
magnificent sight.
Birds and bees
always delight.

Yet the greatest gift
always gives me a lift.
It's you in my heart
'cause we're never apart.

The Cycle

Sunlight following rain

Joy following pain

Loss followed by gain

Over and over again

God-Kissed

What might have been?

Turn your mourning into morning
For I'm living in the GREAT WHAT IS.
Always here, ever near, carrying the Light—
God-Kissed.

True Light

Shadows passing in the night
gone from my earthly sight.
Your gentle whispers in my ear
remind me you are ever near.

You come to me on feathery wings.
What joy thoughts of you do bring!
Your presence, your tender touch
as we meet in the space I love so much.

The light of your being enfolds me here
Washing away my mortal fear
The perils, the pain, the fall from grace
are all erased as I behold your face.

The sky is bright, an azure blue
traveling free, unlimited view.
Your parting reformed me inside out
propelling me beyond all doubt.

Held in a transcendent moment of life
shedding the layers of suffering and strife.
Trusting your light, I step into the Now
before the Eternal, I surrender and bow.

Thank You

Soft caress of the summer breeze
God in this moment
brings me to my knees

This starry night
a gift of love
lifting into the light

Your presence held within my heart
with every breath
never apart

Love Notes

Some days I notice more than others, but you always send love notes. When I *forget,* you open my eyes to the beauty of an autumn day or the brilliant warm glow of an October moon shining in a deep velvet sky. When my ears pick up a tune that makes my heart smile—

I know it's you.

When a friend greets me with a hug, it's you wrapping your arms around me in an ever-present stream of love. Even the deep, sensuous taste of rich dark chocolate on my tongue—yes—it's you reminding me to drink life in, to dance and celebrate every day because we are and will forever be connected in the eternal embrace of our souls.

I feel your whispers in my heart with every beat. Thank you, my Darling Daughter, for blessing me with your presence eternally.

I love you.

SECTION 4

Allowing Grace

A Morning Prayer

This morning you waved as a green leaf dancing in the sunlight.
As I sat in meditation,
you washed over me as a radiant glow.
Now, you are the tears falling on my lips,
turning the edges into a tender smile.
Let me carry your presence out into the world.
Amen.

All Truth Revealed in the One

My beloved child, thank you for your grace—
 for reaching through the clouds of doubt
 for the beauty of your shining face
 for singing me your peace when my soul shouts.

Your love enfolds, whispers, *You are free.*
I rise to greet the morning sun
your words of wisdom let me see
all truth revealed in the One.

I Bow

I watch clouds dance across the sky.
Your smile turns up the corners of my mouth
Embraced by sultry winds,
feet planted on warm grass,
I bow.

The Thinning Veil

I reach across to touch your skin
the veil becoming ever so thin

I step into a world beyond
what I understand in this small pond

The air breathes me in
The mist becomes dim
The Light shines from within

The voice is my own
It welcomes me home

The Next Part of My Journey

Beloved Child, now ageless, eternal, and free—
    your smile enters my heart and moves to my lips.
Your sweet whisper breathes, speaks to me.
What joy your gentle presence brings!
My journey continues—learning you'll welcome me
    home.

Presence

Lifting the receiver, I enter the sacred chamber of my heart.
Quiet, I feel her presence.
Often, she is not alone.
The Light Team gathers.
Angels, known and unknown, touch down.

Energy quickens.
Life surges.
Stillness deepens.
I experience clarity as ideas crystalize from the void,
    —highlighted, defined, no ordinary range of white light—
a frequency so bold and bright, I lose all words
Pure and simple, yet exquisite beyond belief
    —a radiance so magnificent—
my mind is enveloped, enlivened, transported.

A universe infinite, whole, and perfect emerges.
I see beyond mortal eyes, the grand tapestry richly woven
—each thread glows with rich evanescence—
unique and yet, holographically connected
Energy dances in a grand gestalt
a matrix so beautiful
I know I am in the presence of the Divine.

Emotional Labor

The heart seeks to connect self to Self.
Homing, not to a place, but to
   a way of being.
Finding Presence in all things
even pain and sadness,
allowing light to reach into the cave of darkness
returning to the healing peace of love.

Joy/Sorrow

Joy/sorrow—a heartbeat between
the space unseen.
Yet my soul travels the ground
on the wings of the sacred sound.

All held within
for there is no sin.
Only the illusion, the failure to see
it's all One. How else could it be?

Song of My Heart

Let us remember and grieve.
Let us use pain and sorrow to move us into the hope of tomorrow.
Let us hold to faith in goodness and the joy of the present moment.

We don't need to lock up our anger and pain to live in Spirit.
We need only turn on the light, let go of our self-judgment,
    and release our unruly emotions into love.

SECTION 5

The Path Through

Reweaving the Torn Cloth

Healing what once was severed,
holding with loving attention and trust,
we rejoin what was once lost to death unjust.

May we hold the sacred space to reweave the torn cloth—
    To craft from sorrow a new vision of life
    To build and nourish a deep well of compassion
    To create ritual and stories to sustain and teach
    To honor with humility and gratitude what we have been given
    To offer, on bended knee, the prayer of soul connection
    To give thanks for *dark wisdom*
    To acknowledge the Spirit that walks beside us
        as we travel through grief
    To stand on holy ground.

God's secrets

are whispered at the bottom of breaths,
the glimpse of a miracle in the sun-dappled light.

Step into the sea and feel past, present, and future
    as the Oneness of Now
See the tracery of the divine as the midnight sky lights with stars
Taste life's fire on your tongue like hot, rich Mexican chocolate
Inhale the succulent sweetness of jasmine moving from nose
    through body, reaching into the space between breaths
Touch heaven on earth as you caress a baby's downy cheek,
    kiss its tiny, outstretched fingers

Gather life with all your senses and then
surrender, honoring each precious gift
as you let go into love.

On the Shores of Thought

on the shores
of thought
feelings washing over
under, around
words forming
uttering what's felt
in stillness
yet
they cannot capture
the fullness, the secret
sounds of the soul
the place
of perfect Presence
so I rest
in the peace, embraced
lovingly held
in the beauty
in the freedom
of the unnamable world
where all is One

Jewel

Here I am, in this moment
allowing life to flow through me
to be just as it is in all
its flawed abundance,
perfectly present, accepting,
arriving at this place of peace,
this precious jewel of *now*.

Remember Why You Came

Pause a moment
   remember why you came
Breathe in the truth of light
   we are all the same
Beings with hearts,
   embedded in flesh
Carrying earthbound pain.

Look beyond shadows and doubt
   beyond anger, hatred, fear
Return to the love that lies within
   again and again
For God is ever near.

Touching Tranquility

Surveying my inner Self
I touch tranquility.
I know all sentiment, all emotion
while holding the dignity of knowing my soul.

Inner Garden

Tend your inner garden with love,
draw the nourishing light from above.
Seek wisdom with kindness and strength,
your garden will blossom in depth and length.

Angels Leaning In

Life's filled to the brim, with joy, with pain
God waters our spirits with sacred rain
We walk through darkness with anger, fear
The solace we seek is ever near

In the silence, we are blessed
Angels lean in from above
Be still, watch and listen
Learn the truth of His love

Radical Hope

Let me weep not whimper.
Let me be hope.
Let me live from a place of intelligent faith,
  offering compassion from a mother's wisdom.
Knowing the pain but bringing the strength
  of radical hope.
Recognizing future goodness transcending,
  healing present wounds.

Dance with Me

Mystical caravan in the sky
time only exists in the eye.
Homeward bound—below, above
we are held in eternal love.

Imagine now a peace-filled place
The newborness of baby's face
Feel the cast of a magic spell
Joy is where we truly dwell

Join me in the radiance.
Twirl me 'round this thrilling dance.
Set aside the burden of strife.
The time is now, embrace this life!

Surrender

Rising from the ocean's belly
each wave transforms into surf
washing the sand with frothy foam
before returning to the depths
inviting me to surrender
to my own deep source—
    healing my soul
    making me whole

Welcome Home

My heart beats the eternal rhythm and whispers
of the never-broken connection to Home.
Divine tracings, infinite and invisible, are recorded
in my immortal soul, holding me tenderly in all my brokenness.

I will listen and bear witness to the light—the powerful light
infusing even the darkest night with divine beauty. Penetrating
the unravelling force of death, bringing me into communion with
the sweet souls gone before, leading me to the Love that created
us all—

welcoming me Home.

Wings Spread Wide

Come fly with me across the sky
The trees reach up with sun-kissed leaves
The hawk is soaring with wings spread wide
We're held in love and wrapped in light
Our souls will never die

Shine

Light your candle and let it shine—
The world needs you.

You created space inside to hold the world's pain.
Let your heart transfigure it into needed wisdom—bring it!
Share the Presence.

Guidance

Enter the place of stillness, a place beyond words.
Break through fear and worry to a state of deep connection.
Surrender to the allness of Love.

Doubts will dissolve into knowing that all stands in Divine order.
Each emergence will bring more and more awareness into life—
daily.
Let that Love guide you in all things.

God guides in stillness—listen!

When the heart grieves over what it has lost,
the spirit cherishes what it has kept.
—Sufi wisdom

Acknowledgments

I am grateful for:

Larry Glasscock, my loving husband who walks this healing journey with me daily.

Mike Glasscock, my amazing son and Carrie's big brother, whose own journey with cancer is a testimony to his strength and courage.

Brian West, Carrie's devoted husband, who cared for her with undying love and tenderness.

Barbara Lewis West, Carrie's dear mother-in-law, who loved her with the heart of a big sister and never gave up.

Dr. Colleen Cecilia Brown, Carrie's dear friend and the doctor who steadfastly walked her home.

Dr. Anna Maria Storniolo, Carrie's amazing oncologist who showered her with incredible care, friendship, and love.

Iva Nasr, my dear friend and author who taught my broken heart how to listen.

Dr. Katie Pedersen, dedicated pediatrician and Carrie's loving friend who keeps Carrie's memory alive in the hearts and prayers of her children.

Dr. Greg Gramelspacher, Carrie's mentor and friend who supported and cared for her during, not only her medical training, but her final journey home.

Libby Brown, my faithful friend whose heart-to-heart hugs saw me through some of my darkest days and whose technical skills brought these poems out of my journals and into a Word document.

Rhonda Green, whose own courageous journey added encouragement for these poems to be shared.

Lucy, the little soul who donned the body of a mini dachshund so she could be born into the world when Carrie needed a spirit to be her constant companion as she walked her path through cancer.

I couldn't close these pages without thanking the two amazing women who turned my journal entries into a book that could be sent into the world. It is with deep gratitude for their understanding, expertise, and nurturing support that I acknowledge Carrie Jareed and Karen Burton. Thank you.

Finally, I am grateful for all the loving friends and family who nurtured, supported, held, and breathed life back into my soul as I walked through the many valleys toward the healing Light.

All who grieve. May you find comfort.

About the Author

Lee Glasscock is a wife, mother, grandmother. She and her husband Larry live in Florida and Indiana. Originally from Ohio, she worked as a therapist at The Women's Center in Vienna, Virginia, after relocating to the Washington, DC area. The couple, along with their son, daughter, and their spouses formed a family foundation in 2007, funding education, cancer research, and food insecurity relief.

Before she passed, their daughter Carrie became part of a grassroots organization: *100 Voices of Hope*, a source of funding and inspiration for breast cancer researchers. Carrie's passion to support and grow this endeavor was contagious, and The Glasscock Family Foundation has been privileged to join in this extraordinary ongoing effort.

Lee is passionate about her family, friends, and books. Her heart's desire is to never stop learning or growing and to stay open to life.

www.ingramcontent.com/pod-product-compliance
Lightning Source LLC
Chambersburg PA
CBHW061704120626
46550CB00003B/1087